OUR GALAXY AND BEYOND

MERCURY

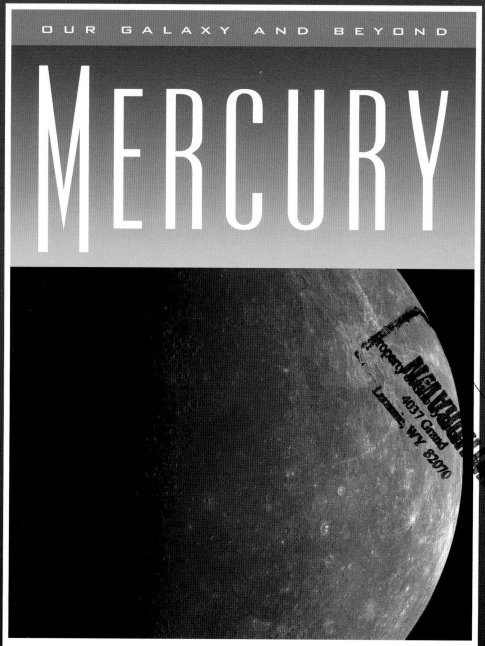

By Darlene R. Stille

The Child's World®

Published in the United States of America by The Child's World®
P.O. Box 326, Chanhassen, MN 55317-0326
800-599-READ
www.childsworld.com

Photo Credits: Cover: NASA/JPL/Caltech/Northwestern University; Corbis: 5, 6 (Araldo de Luca), 7, 12, 16, 17 (Nation Wong), 18 (Werner H. Müller), 20 (Vittoriano Rastelli), 22, 25 (Myron Jay Dorf); NASA/JPL/Caltech: 8, 10 (GSFC/LaRC/MISR Team), 13, 14 (Arizona State University), 15, 19 (USGS), 21, 27, 31; NASA/SOHO: 23; Reuters NewMedia Inc./Corbis: 24, 26; Roger Ressmeyer/Corbis: 9, 11 (NASA).

The Child's World®: Mary Berendes, Publishing Director
Editorial Directions, Inc.: E. Russell Primm, Editorial Director; Dana Rau, Line Editor; Elizabeth K. Martin, Assistant Editor; Olivia Nellums, Editorial Assistant; Susan Hindman, Copy Editor; Susan Ashley, Proofreader; Kevin Cunningham, Peter Garnham, Chris Simms, Fact Checkers; Tim Griffin/IndexServ, Indexer; Cian Loughlin O'Day, Photo Researcher; Linda S. Koutris, Photo Selector

*Content Adviser:
Michelle Nichols,
Lead Educator for
Informal Programs,
Adler Planetarium
& Astronomy
Museum, Chicago,
Illinois*

Library of Congress Cataloging-in-Publication Data
Stille, Darlene R.
  Mercury / by Darlene Stille.
     p. cm. — (Our galaxy and beyond)
Summary: Introduces the planet Mercury, exploring its atmosphere, composition, and other characteristics and looking particularly at how humans learned about the planet closest to the sun. Includes bibliographical references and index.
  ISBN 1-59296-051-0 (lib. bdg. : alk. paper)
  1. Mercury (Planet)—Juvenile literature. [1. Mercury (Planet)] I. Title. II. Series.
  QB611.S75 2004
  523.41—dc21   2003006333

TABLE OF CONTENTS

CHAPTER ONE

DISCOVERING MERCURY

Mercury is one of nine planets in our solar system that orbits, or goes around, the Sun. It is the closest planet to the Sun. We know less about Mercury than any other planet except Pluto. The Sun's glare is one reason we know so little about Mercury. The Sun is very bright. You can't look at the Sun. It would hurt your eyes. The glare of the Sun makes anything near it hard to see.

Mercury is also hard to see because it is tiny. It is about half the size of Earth. Mercury is the second smallest planet in our solar system. Pluto is the smallest. We can only see Mercury for a short time just before sunrise and just after sunset.

Since the 1800s, **astronomers** have tried to learn how Mercury moves in space. Mercury has an oval-shaped orbit around the

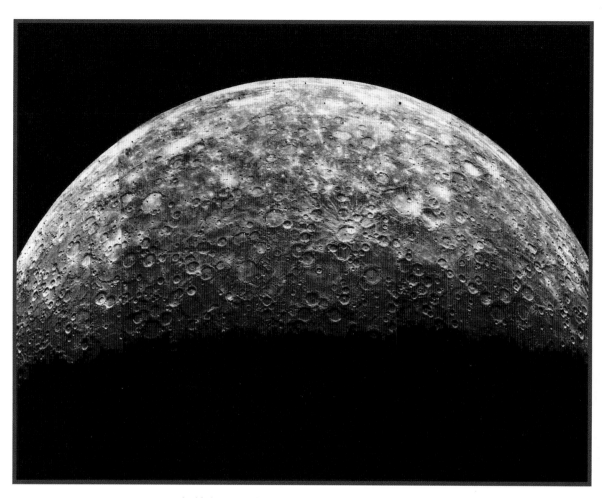

Mercury is one half the size of Earth and Venus, and is much less colorful, too.

Sun. Because of its long, oval orbit, Mercury is sometimes close to the Sun and is sometimes farther away.

Mercury orbits the Sun faster than any other planet. It only takes Mercury 88 Earth-days to go around the Sun once. Mercury travels at about 30 miles (48 kilometers) per second. The planet was named after

The swift Roman god Mercury was also known as Hermes by the Greeks.

the swift messenger of the ancient Roman gods. Mercury had wings on his heels to help him move quickly.

Mercury may orbit the Sun quickly, but it turns very slowly. It takes Earth 24 hours to make one turn on its axis. An axis is an imaginary line going through the center of a planet. A planet spins around its axis. One turn around Earth's axis is one Earth-day. In 1965, astronomers found that it takes Mercury 59 Earth-days to make one turn around its axis.

Only one spacecraft has visited Mercury. The spacecraft was named *Mariner 10*. *Mariner 10* was an unmanned space **probe.** This means that it did not carry a pilot or astronauts. Instead, it

Mariner 10 *flew almost 470 miles (756 km) above Mercury and took photographs of nearly half of the planet's surface.*

carried cameras to take pictures. It also carried instruments to do tests

or take measurements.

Mariner 10 flew past Mercury twice, once in 1974 and again

in 1975. Each time it flew past Mercury, its cameras clicked away.

Mariner 10 took thousands of pictures of Mercury. The pictures

showed about half of Mercury's surface.

Astronomers are still studying the *Mariner 10* pictures. They also look at Mercury with radar or with special kinds of **telescopes** called radio telescopes. They are trying different ways to learn more about this tiny planet that is so close to the Sun.

This image, called a photomosaic, was created from dozens of the photographs taken by Mariner 10. *Like a jigsaw puzzle, the separate shots of Mercury's surface had to be matched correctly to create the whole picture.*

Mercury is hard to see with telescopes that use ordinary light. But astronomers have learned how to "see" in space with **radio waves.** They use a special telescope called a radio telescope.

A radio telescope looks like a TV satellite dish, but it is much bigger. The world's largest and most powerful radio telescope dish is at the Arecibo Observatory in Puerto Rico. The dish is 1,000 feet (305 meters) across. The Very Large Array is the name of a different type of radio telescope. It has 27 satellite dishes. Each dish is 82 feet (25 m) in diameter. All 27 dishes can work together to pick up radio signals. The Very Large Array is near Socorro, New Mexico.

There are different types of radio signals. Radar is one type of radio signal. The word stands for Radio Detecting And Ranging. Radar can help people see through the dark. It can see through clouds and fog, so it helps airplanes fly and land safely. Radar even helps predict the weather.

Radar works by sending out a radio beam. If the beam hits something, it bounces back. Then a radio telescope picks up the bouncing beam. Computers use the beam to make patterns on radar screens.

Astronomers bounced radio beams off Mercury and measured the time it took the signals to return. This helped them make maps of Mercury's surface. It helped show that there may be ice at Mercury's north and south poles. Radar also helped astronomers learn that Mercury has almost no atmosphere.

CHAPTER TWO

MERCURY'S ATMOSPHERE

An atmosphere is the layer of gases that surrounds a planet.

Earth's atmosphere is responsible for our weather and for keeping

us safe from the Sun's hot rays. At first, astronomers thought that

*Earth's atmosphere is much different than that of Mercury.
Here, a snowstorm brews over the eastern United States.*

Mercury had no atmosphere at all! Then, they discovered a tiny amount of helium and a few other gases around Mercury.

The rough, gray surface of Mercury experiences huge variations in temperature from day to night.

Heat trapped in a planet's atmosphere during the day can help keep that planet warm at night. On Mercury, however, there is not enough gas to trap heat from the Sun. This makes Mercury's temperatures swing wildly from high to low. Mercury is so close to the Sun that its daytime temperatures soar to more than 809° Fahrenheit (432° Celsius). This is hot enough to melt lead metal! But because it has so little atmosphere, Mercury's nighttime temperatures drop to about –292° F (–180° C).

THE BLACK SKY OF MERCURY

Mercury's sky looks very different from our sky on Earth. The sky above Mercury always looks dark. Even in the daytime, Mercury's sky looks like the nighttime sky above Earth. Why do the two skies look so different? The answer has to do with the differences in their atmospheres.

A planet's atmosphere is what makes the sky look a certain color. Light from the Sun comes toward the planet in a straight line. As it moves through the planet's atmosphere, however, rays of sunlight strike **molecules** of gas. The light then bounces off in a new direction. This is called scattering.

Sunlight looks white, but really it contains light in all the colors of the rainbow. The light travels in waves, like water in an ocean. The color of the light depends on the size of the wave, or the wavelength. Earth's atmosphere scatters more of the light that has shorter wavelengths. Blue wavelengths are short, so the gas molecules in our atmosphere scatter more blue rays toward us than those of other colors. That is why the sky usually looks blue from Earth. But Mercury does not have enough of an atmosphere to scatter rays from the Sun. So Mercury's sky always looks black.

CHAPTER THREE

WHAT MERCURY IS MADE OF

Mercury looks a lot like Earth's Moon. Mercury is gray, dry, and covered with large, bowl-shaped holes called craters. The craters on Mercury are all sizes. Some are very small. Others are up to 800 miles (1,300 km) across. **Comets** or **meteorites** crashing into

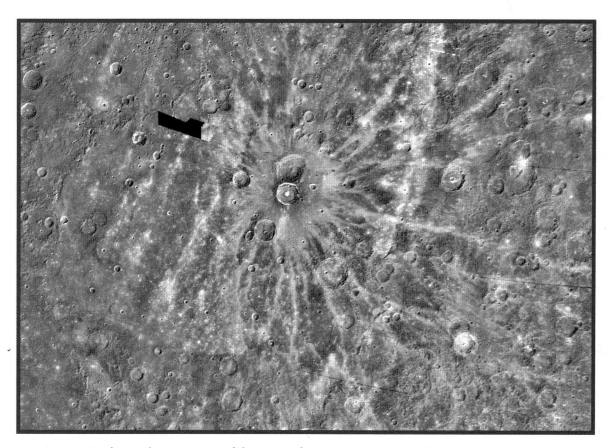

Bright streaks coming out of the center of a crater are a common feature on Mercury.

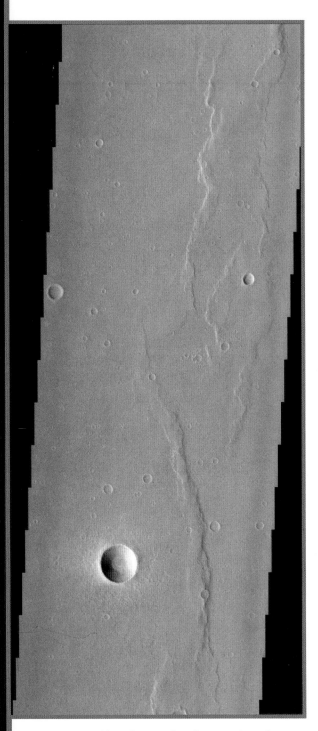

Craters, wrinkle ridges, and wide, smoother plains are all part of Mercury's hard surface terrain. Craters as small as 500 feet (150 m) across can be seen in this high resolution image taken by Mariner 10.

Mercury made the craters.

Some of Mercury's craters

have bright lines that look

like rays coming out from

the center. Some craters have

a peak in the middle.

Mercury also has wrin-

kles all over its surface. They

are called wrinkle ridges.

What made the wrinkles?

Scientists think the inside of

Mercury may have cooled

and grown smaller. The sur-

face would have been too

big for the inside of the planet. The loose surface may have wrinkled.

Even though Mercury gets very hot, there is frozen water on Mercury. The ice is in craters at the planet's poles.

Scientists changed the colors in this image to show more clearly the cloud-like "comma" surrounding the center of the comet Borrelly. Mercury seems to have been bombarded by meteorites and perhaps some icy comets.

It lies in cold, deep shadows at the bottom of the craters. Scientists do not think that there was ever a large amount of water on this hot, dry planet. Instead, they think icy comets may have crashed into Mercury and made the craters. The ice from the comets stayed frozen at the bottom of these deep holes.

Mercury is a very dense planet. Density is the amount of matter in an object. Mercury is almost as dense as Earth, even though it is much smaller. A dense metal called iron makes up a large part of Mercury. The planet probably has a core, or center, made mostly of iron. A layer of rock called the mantle surrounds the core. On top of the mantle is the rocky crust and surface of Mercury.

Mercury's rocky landscape includes many craters with peaks rising from their centers.

CHAPTER FOUR

MERCURY'S MAGNETIC FIELD

Mariner 10 discovered that Mercury has a weak magnetic

field. A magnetic field is the area around a magnet where its pull

can be felt. You can feel the pull of a magnet when you hold it

close to a refrigerator door. The magnet tries to "stick" to the

door. Mercury's magnetic field sur-

rounds the planet and goes

out into space.

Earth has a magnetic

field, too. Earth spins rap-

idly and has an iron core.

There are two parts to Earth's

core. The inner core is

The magnetic needle inside a compass always points north because of Earth's strong magnetic field. Mercury's weak magnetism probably wouldn't have much effect on a compass needle.

solid iron. The outer core is melted, liquid iron. Scientists think the

spinning liquid iron is what turns Earth into a giant magnet.

The magnetic field around Mercury was a surprise to scientists.

They had thought only big planets that spin quickly, such as Earth,

could act as magnets. But Mercury is a small planet that turns slowly.

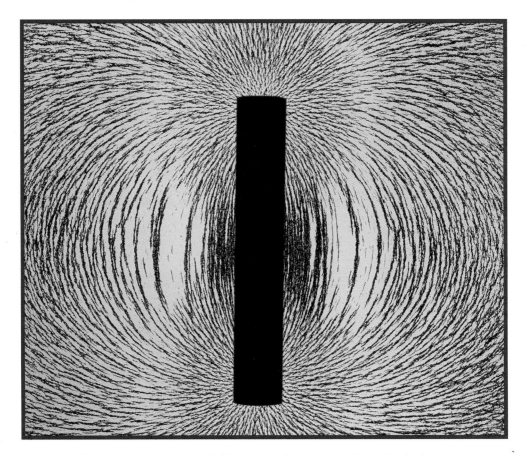

*Iron filings within a magnetic field are strongly drawn to the ends of a bar magnet.
Planets with an iron core, such as Mercury and Earth, also have magnetic fields.*

*Beneath its hard, cratered crust, Mercury may be
hiding a spinning core of hot liquid iron.*

So what turns Mercury into a magnet? Scientists think that to

be a magnet, Mercury must be made mostly of iron. They believe

that an iron core makes up most of Mercury. Some of that iron

must be hot, spinning liquid, like Earth's inner core.

CHAPTER FIVE

Mercury's Ancient Volcanoes

Mercury looks gray and quiet today. But in the past, fountains of hot melted rock may have erupted out of active **volcanoes.** Fiery rivers of melted rock, called lava, may have flowed across its surface. The lava came from oceans of melted rock inside the planet.

Rivers of fiery lava probably helped shape Mercury's terrain, just as they have in some places on Earth.

Mariner 10 pictures showed that some craters on Mercury have smooth bottoms. There are also large flat areas on Mercury. Volcanoes could have made these areas.

Scientists think lava erupting out of volcanoes flowed over large

parts of the planet. Then it cooled and hardened. It made smooth

layers on the floors of craters. It made the large flat areas that look

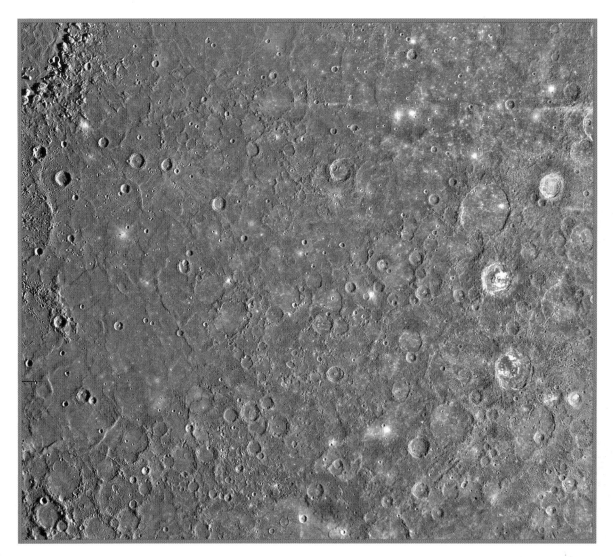

Scientists suspect that the plains on Mercury were created from lava
that flowed over the planet and then cooled and hardened.

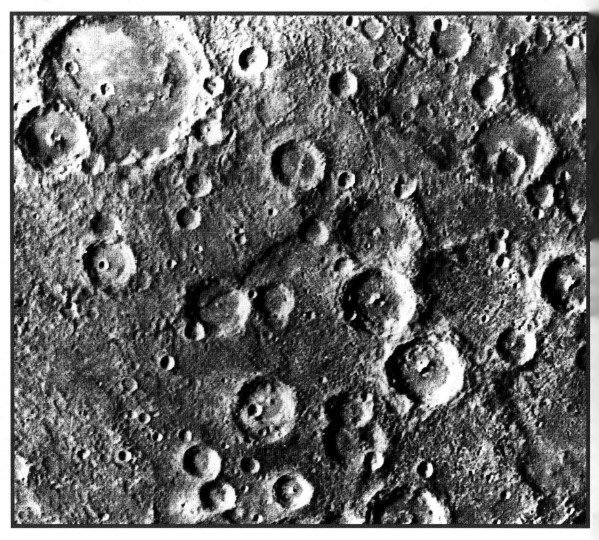

Craters of all sizes dot the plains of Mercury.

like plains. Places that look like lava flows seem to be made of different chemicals than the rest of the surface.

To find out if lava once flowed across Mercury, scientists must send more spacecraft to study the planet more closely.

MERCURY'S HOT POLES

Like other planets, Mercury has a north pole and a south pole. These poles are at the top and bottom of the planet. They are the coldest spots on the planet. Mercury also has two "hot poles." The hot poles are at its equator. The equator is an imaginary line that goes around the middle of the planet. Once every Mercury-year, a certain spot on the planet's equator is the closest part of the planet to the Sun. The next Mercury-year, the spot on the opposite side of the equator is closest to the Sun. Rays from the Sun make the spots roasting hot. Scientists named these opposite spots along the equator Mercury's hot poles.

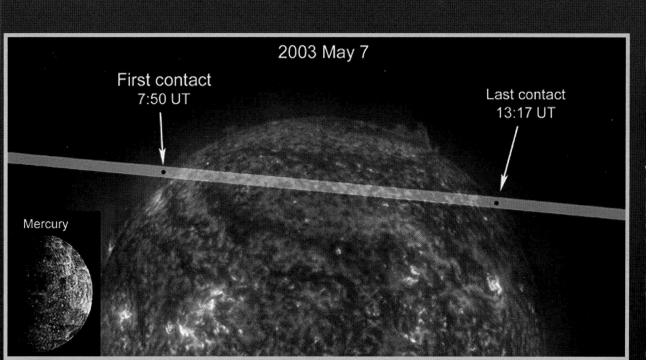

2003 May 7

First contact
7:50 UT

Last contact
13:17 UT

Mercury

CHAPTER SIX

HOW MERCURY
MAY HAVE FORMED

Astronomers want to know how Mercury formed. They believe

the solar system began as a cloud of dust and gas spinning around the

Sun. All the planets formed from material in that cloud. Astronomers

have two ideas about how Mercury was formed.

Mercury was born from a spinning cloud of dust and gas,
but scientists disagree about how it actually formed.

According to one idea, Mercury formed in the hottest part of the spinning cloud near the Sun that contained lots of rock and metal. The hot material came together to form a planet

Like all the planets in the solar system, Mercury is part of a huge cluster of stars and other matter called the Milky Way galaxy, as shown here.

that was mostly made of iron metal. The planet cooled. The heavy iron sank to the center. The iron now is in Mercury's core. This left thin layers of rocky crust and mantle around the core.

The other idea is that Mercury formed from pieces of rock that came from farther away in the solar system. The pieces stuck together to form a planet. Then, a huge comet or an **asteroid** struck the planet. The crash blew off much of Mercury's outer rock

An artist imagines what the crash of an asteroid into a planet might look like.

layer. Mercury was left with its large iron core.

Another mission to Mercury may help scientists decide which idea is correct. The next robot spacecraft going to Mercury is called *MESSENGER*. It is scheduled for launch in 2004. The *MESSENGER* spacecraft will fly past Mercury in 2008 and go into orbit around the planet in 2009.

MESSENGER will find out what the surface of Mercury is made of. It will study the magnetic field and look for more clues about the planet's core and atmosphere. If *MESSENGER* finds little or no iron in the soil and rocks on Mercury, it could mean all the iron is in its core. This would support the idea that Mercury formed near the Sun. If the spacecraft finds iron in the rocks and soil, it could mean Mercury formed from material that came from elsewhere in the solar system.

Scientists believe that this little planet can tell them much about the early solar system. How did melting inside the planets help form their crusts, mantles, and cores? Mercury may hold many clues to what it was like when the planets first formed.

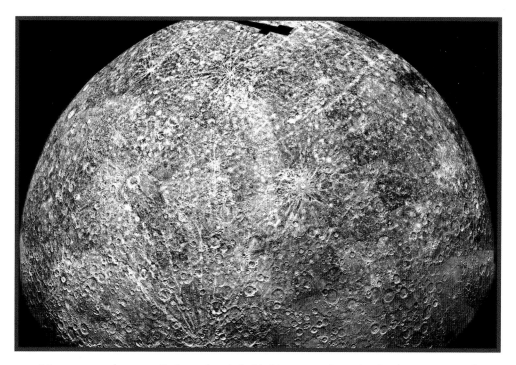

Mercury may be a small planet but it holds big secrets that scientists hope to unravel.

Glossary

asteroid (ASS-tuh-royd) An asteroid is a rocky object that orbits the Sun.

astronomers (uh-STRAW-nuh-merz) Astronomers are scientists who study space, the stars, and the planets.

comets (KOM-its) Comets are bright objects, followed by tails of dust and ice, that orbit the Sun in long, oval-shaped paths.

meteorites (MEE-tee-uh-rites) Meteorites are rocky or metallic objects from space that hit the surface of a planet.

molecules (MOL-uh-kyools) Molecules are the smallest parts of a substance that still have all the characteristics of the larger substance.

probe (PROBE) A probe is a machine or tool that explores something.

radio waves (RAY-dee-oh WAVES) Radio waves are a type of electromagnetic wave that travels through space.

telescopes (TEL-uh-skopes) Telescopes are instruments used to study things that are far away, such as stars and planets, by making them seem larger and closer.

volcanoes (vol-KAY-nose) Volcanoes are mountains that contain an opening in the surface of a planet. When a volcano erupts, melted rock from pools of magma below the surface spews from the top.

Did You Know?

▸ *Mariner 10* is still orbiting the Sun, but rays from the Sun have probably destroyed all of its controls.

▸ Many meteors burn up in Earth's atmosphere before they can strike our planet. Burning meteors are sometimes called shooting stars. Mercury has almost no atmosphere, so meteors do not burn up. They crash into the planet and are called meteorites.

▶ For a long time, astronomers thought the same side of Mercury always faced the Sun. This would be true if Mercury turned once every time it made one orbit. But in 1965, they discovered that Mercury makes three full turns on its axis for every two times it goes around the Sun. It just so happens that every time Mercury comes closest to Earth, we see the same side of the planet.

▶ The Caloris Basin is the largest single feature that we can see on Mercury. The Caloris Basin is a crater that was probably made by a large meteorite. It is about 800 miles (1,300 km) across.

Fast Facts

Diameter: 3,032 miles (4,880 km)

Atmosphere: helium, hydrogen, oxygen, sodium, potassium

Time to orbit the Sun (one Mercury-year): 88 Earth-days

Time to turn on axis (one Mercury-day): 58.6 Earth-days

Average distance from the Sun: 36 million miles (58 million km)

Shortest distance from the Sun: 29 million miles (46 million km)

Greatest distance from the Sun: 43 million miles (70 million km)

Shortest distance from Earth: 48 million miles (77 million km)

Greatest distance from Earth: 138 million miles (222 million km)

Surface gravity: 0.38 that of Earth. A person weighing 80 pounds (36 kg) on Earth would weigh about 30 pounds (14 kg) on Mercury.

Temperature range: −292° F (−180° C) during the day to 809° F (432° C) at night

Number of known moons: 0

How to Learn More about Mercury

At the Library

Asimov, Isaac, and Richard Hantula. *Mercury.* Milwaukee: Gareth Stevens, 2002.

Cole, Michael D. *Mercury: The First Planet.* Berkeley Heights, N.J.: Enslow, 2001.

Goss, Tim. *Mercury.* Chicago: Heinemann Library, 2002.

Spangenburg, Ray. *A Look at Mercury.* New York: Franklin Watts, 2003.

Stone, Tanya Lee. *Mercury.* New York: Benchmark Books, 2002.

On the Web

Visit our home page for lots of links about Mercury:
http://www.childsworld.com/links.html
Note to Parents, Teachers, and Librarians: We routinely verify our Web links to
make sure they're safe, active sites—so encourage your readers to check them out!

Through the Mail or by Phone

ADLER PLANETARIUM AND ASTRONOMY MUSEUM
1300 South Lake Shore Drive
Chicago, IL 60605-2403
312/922-STAR

NATIONAL AIR AND SPACE MUSEUM
7th and Independence Avenue, S.W.
Washington, DC 20560
202/357-2700

LUNAR AND PLANETARY INSTITUTE
3600 Bay Area Boulevard
Houston, TX 77058
281/486-2139

The solar system

Index

About the Author

Darlene R. Stille is a science writer. She has lived in Chicago, Illinois, all her life. When she was in high school, she fell in love with science. While attending the University of Illinois she discovered that she also loved writing. She was fortunate to find a career that allowed her to combine both her interests. Darlene Stille has written about 60 books for young people.